How true are the words of a lover?
How promising are the promises to
one another?

Love. is in the air. It's only those who believes in it, get to smell it fragrances.

While we may not always find it, how we want to, it surely come when we least expect it.

Let's travel through the pages of this little piece into a realm where patience was tried, love was tested and how something that seems not meant to be, brought one to the path of fulfillment.

LET'S DIG IN!

Here I find myself, engulfed in a profound melancholy, grappling with the existential query of whether love truly exists. Amidst the tumultuous sea of emotions, I am torn between embracing the tangible affection offered to me and succumbing to the mere semblance of it. Casting my gaze into the distance, my eyes chance upon a pair of lovers, their laughter echoing through the air as they revel in each other's company. Is that the essence of love, I ponder inwardly? And in that moment of introspection, a haunting uncertainty grips me: am I standing at a distance from love, or is love elusively evading my grasp?

Suddenly, a brisk, wintry gust swept through the surroundings, stirring up a delicate dance of dust and leaves that twirled gracefully in the air. Amidst this ephemeral display of nature's whims, my attention was captivated by a melodic tweet emanating from the branches above. To my delight, a mesmerizing tableau unfolded before my eyes – two avian creatures, adorned in the splendor of their plumage, engrossed in an enchanting exchange of glances. It was evident that a lighthearted spectacle was unfurling, an interplay of avian mirth and camaraderie. In the symphony of their tweets, one could almost perceive a serenade, a harmonious composition woven in the delicate threads of their feathered connection.

As I beheld this enchanting scene unfolding before me, a glimmer of hope ignited within my heart. Perhaps, I mused to myself, these harmonious interactions between the birds were a testament to the existence of true love. This newfound perspective infused me with a sense of optimism, casting aside the shadows of doubt that had clouded my mind. With renewed faith in the mysterious workings of fate, I whispered to myself, "Maybe love will find me when the stars align, or perhaps I'll stumble upon it when the time is ripe." Casting another wistful glance towards the distant couple, a gentle smile graced my lips, illuminating my face with a warmth that mirrored the beauty of the moment. Indeed, it was a sublime experience, a reminder that amidst life's uncertainties, love's enduring presence remains a beacon of possibility and joy.

As the day gradually surrendered to the embrace of twilight, the once serene sky now painted itself with hues of somber gray, hinting at the impending arrival of nightfall. Yet, despite the encroaching darkness, I rose from my reverie with a renewed sense of positivity enveloping me like a comforting shroud. With each step homeward, I traversed the bustling streets, weaving through the throngs of fellow travelers, lost in a wistful reverie of the love I yearned to discover.

In my mind's eye, I envisioned a tapestry of romantic delights awaiting me: the delicate fragrance of blossoming flowers, the indulgent sweetness of chocolate shared between lovers, the tender caress of a kiss exchanged in the soft glow of moonlight, and the harmonious symphony of laughter echoing through the night. With each passing moment, my anticipation swelled, like a crescendo building towards the climax of an enchanting symphony.

As I journeyed homeward, my thoughts were consumed by fantasies of love's embrace, each daydream a testament to the boundless depths of my longing. For in the tapestry of life, woven with threads of hope and desire, I awaited the arrival of that great and wondrous experience - the discovery of true love.

Allow me to introduce myself - I am Emily, a spirited young woman brimming with ambition and dreams. Nestled within the quaint confines of the small city of Villet, I share a humble abode with my devoted aunt, whose days are tirelessly dedicated to the artistry of baking within her bustling bakery.

Oh, how I yearn to lend a hand in crafting those delectable cakes and pastries that beckon tantalizingly from the display cases! Yet, despite my eager pleas and earnest desire to immerse myself in the aromatic wonders of the bakery, my aunt remains resolute in her insistence that my studies take precedence. And so, I find solace in the realm of academia, dedicating ample time to searching and researching, in pursuit of knowledge and enlightenment.

Yet, amidst the intellectual pursuits that occupy my days, there exists a palpable void - a longing for something elusive and intangible. Love. The absence of companionship weighs heavily upon my heart, as I navigate the corridors of my school, surrounded by a sea of faces, yet feeling adrift and disconnected. Although the schoolyard teems with boys, forging meaningful connections with them feels akin to a daunting task, leaving me feeling somewhat out of place and disconcerted in their presence.

Thus, I find myself caught betwixt the realms of academia and the yearnings of the heart, longing for the warmth of friendship and the tender embrace of love, yet unsure of how to bridge the chasm that separates me from these elusive desires.

Upon my bookshelf, an array of novels and self-help tomes stand proudly, their spines adorned with promises of unlocking the secrets to finding true love. Yet, despite my fervent perusal of their pages, the elusive essence of love remains tantalizingly out of reach. With each passing day, the weight of my eighteen years upon this earth bears down upon me, casting shadows of doubt upon the possibility of ever finding a boyfriend, of experiencing that tender connection that so many around me seem to effortlessly embrace.

However, in the wake of the serendipitous encounter with the birds and the enamored couple, a newfound sense of hope blossoms within me like a delicate flower pushing through hardened soil. It is as though the universe itself has whispered words of reassurance, reminding me that true love is not bound by the constraints of time or circumstance, but rather, it unfurls its wings in the most unexpected of moments, soaring effortlessly into the hearts of those who dare to believe.

And so, buoyed by this newfound sense of optimism, I cast aside the weight of my doubts and fears, embracing the belief that love, in its purest form, will inevitably find its way to me. For in the tapestry of life, woven with threads of destiny and serendipity, I trust that my own journey towards love is but a chapter waiting to be written, filled with the promise of joy, companionship, and the sweetest of romances.

As seconds stretched into minutes, and minutes morphed into hours, Emily's hope soared skyward like a brightly colored kite dancing amidst the clouds. With each passing day, she eagerly anticipated the arrival of true love, believing with unwavering conviction that destiny would soon lead her into the arms of her soulmate. Days melted into weeks, and weeks seamlessly flowed into months, yet despite her earnest efforts to be present in every moment, the elusive touch of love remained just beyond her grasp.

With each passing disappointment, Emily couldn't help but question her own existence in the realm of love. Am I invisible? she pondered, her heart heavy with uncertainty. Despite her valiant attempts to remain optimistic, the flickering flame of hope began to dim, its once vibrant glow fading into the shadows of doubt and despair.

Sinking into a contemplative silence, Emily found herself engulfed in a sea of introspection, grappling with the age-old question of why love had yet to find its way to her. Lost in her thoughts, she was startled by the sound of a gentle greeting – "Hello."

Startled from her reverie, Emily's heart skipped a beat as she turned to face the source of the unexpected salutation, her eyes alighting upon a figure standing before her, their gaze filled with warmth and kindness. In that fleeting moment, amidst the quiet solitude of her contemplation, Emily sensed the stirrings of possibility, a glimmer of hope reigniting within her like a beacon in the darkness. For perhaps, just perhaps, love had been patiently waiting to find her all along.

Emily's breath caught in her throat as she beheld the sight before her – a strikingly charming man, his eyes ablaze with a captivating allure that seemed to draw her in with an irresistible magnetism. With each inhalation, the air around her filled with the intoxicating scent of a myriad of roses, enveloping her senses in a heady whirlwind of passion and desire.

As her gaze swept over his well-defined physique, a rush of exhilaration surged through her veins, transporting her to a realm of fantastical wonder where dreams intertwined with reality. In that fleeting moment, she found herself suspended in a reverie, lost amidst the labyrinth of her imagination, envisioning a love story unfolding before her very eyes.

The air crackled with an electric energy, charged with the palpable anticipation of a love that transcended the boundaries of time and space. In this enchanted realm, two souls found themselves inexorably drawn towards one another, their hearts beating in synchrony as they embarked upon a journey of passion and romance.

In the midst of this ethereal encounter, Emily felt as though she had stumbled upon a treasure trove of possibilities, a kaleidoscope of emotions swirling around her like a whirlwind of emotions. For in the presence of this enigmatic stranger, she sensed the unmistakable stirrings of love, beckoning her to surrender herself to its enchanting embrace.

Then came another "hellooo". The echo of the greeting reverberated through Emily's ears, jolting her back to the present moment as she grappled to regain her composure. With a nervous smile playing upon her lips, she returned the salutation, her heart racing with a mixture of anticipation and uncertainty.

As the young man spoke her name, a furrow formed upon Emily's brow, her mind racing to make sense of the familiarity that lingered in the air. "Can't you remember me?" he inquired, his voice laced with a gentle curiosity that stirred something deep within her.

With a faint nod, Emily acknowledged her identity, her thoughts whirling as she attempted to unravel the enigma before her. Memories flickered like candle flames in the recesses of her mind, fragments of encounters and fleeting glimpses of faces intermingling in a tapestry of recollection.

Suddenly, like a bolt of lightning illuminating the darkness, a spark of recognition ignited within Emily's consciousness, casting light upon the shadowy corridors of her memory. And as clarity dawned upon her, her features softened with realization, her gaze meeting his with a newfound understanding.

Emily's heart sank as the pieces of the puzzle fell into place, revealing the identity of the enigmatic stranger before her. The resemblance to her late uncle was uncanny, a bittersweet reminder of a beloved family member who had departed this world far too soon.

With a heavy heart, Emily tentatively voiced the question that lingered on the tip of her tongue, her voice barely above a whisper, "You are Kelly?"

The young man's laughter filled the air, a melodic symphony that echoed with a haunting familiarity. "Yes," he exclaimed, his eyes alight with amusement at the revelation.

In that moment, the fragile tendrils of hope that had taken root within Emily's soul began to unravel, their delicate fibers unraveling in the face of this unexpected twist of fate. She attempted to mask her disappointment with a forced smile, her heart aching with the weight of unspoken sorrow.

As the two settled into conversation, reminiscing about times long past, Emily found herself grappling with a myriad of emotions swirling within her. Confusion mingled with longing, as she struggled to reconcile the reality of the present with the echoes of the past that reverberated through her soul.

In the quietude of their conversation, amidst the laughter and the shared memories, Emily found herself wrestling with a thousand unanswered questions, each one a poignant reminder of the fragility of life and the unpredictable nature of destiny. And as she sought solace in the embrace of nostalgia, she couldn't help but wonder what might have been, if only fate had chosen to tread a different path.

As the sun dipped below the horizon, casting long shadows across the landscape, Emily felt a sense of finality settling over the encounter that had unfolded before her. Another chapter had come to an end, yet the elusive specter of love still eluded her grasp.

With a heavy heart, Emily and Kelly reluctantly prepared to part ways, the weight of unspoken words hanging in the air between them. As they exchanged numbers and made tentative promises to stay in touch, a hollow ache settled within Emily's chest, a poignant reminder of the fleeting nature of connections forged in the crucible of circumstance.

With a bittersweet smile, Kelly bid her farewell, his parting words echoing softly in the recesses of her mind like a haunting melody. Promises of future visits and fleeting moments of companionship offered a glimmer of solace amidst the darkness of disappointment, yet Emily couldn't shake the gnawing sense of longing that lingered within her soul.

As the scene faded into memory, the worrisome specter of disappointment enveloped Emily once more, casting a shadow over her hopes and dreams of finding true love. Yet amidst the turmoil of emotions that churned within her, a flicker of resilience ignited within her heart, a silent vow to persevere in the face of adversity and to never relinquish the pursuit of happiness and fulfillment.

For Emily knew that although this chapter may have ended in uncertainty and disappointment, the story of her life was far from over. And as she gazed into the unknown expanse of the future, she vowed to seize each moment with courage and determination, trusting that love, in its infinite wisdom, would one day find its way to her.

In the tranquil embrace of an early morning, as the gentle caress of the breeze kissed her cheeks, Emily made the conscious decision to embark on a journey of rejuvenation, both for her body and her spirit. With each rhythmic stride along the familiar path, she sought to shed the burdens of stress and fatigue that had accumulated within her weary frame.

As she jogged gracefully amidst the verdant surroundings, Emily found herself amidst a bustling throng of fellow exercisers, their presence a testament to the shared pursuit of health and vitality. Despite the camaraderie that permeated the air, Emily felt a sense of detachment, a solitary figure lost amidst the sea of bustling activity.

A wave of exhaustion washed over her, prompting Emily to seek respite in the comforting embrace of a shaded alcove. As she sat, her breath ragged and labored, a slender figure approached, his demeanor warm and genial. "Hey, good morning," he greeted with a friendly smile, his voice a gentle melody amidst the quietude of the morning.

Though his intentions were benign, Emily found herself hesitating, her guard raised against the unfamiliar intrusion into her solitude. Despite his attempts to engage her in conversation, she remained distant and aloof, her thoughts consumed by the solitary rhythm of her own existence.

In the end, unable to bridge the chasm that separated them, Emily offered a curt dismissal, her polite refusal a shield against the vulnerability of connection. With a resigned sigh, the man retreated, leaving Emily to her solitary musings as she resumed her exercise with renewed determination.

In the quiet moments that followed the encounter, Emily found herself grappling with a torrent of emotions that swirled tumultuously within her. The lingering sense of unease gnawed at her conscience, a relentless reminder of the possibility she may have overlooked in her haste to retreat into solitude.

Day and night, the memory of their brief interaction played on a loop in her mind, each replay accompanied by a pang of regret for the opportunity that may have slipped through her fingers. Was she too quick to shut the door on the possibility of connection, she wondered, her thoughts a whirlwind of uncertainty and self-doubt.

Despite her attempts to bury the encounter beneath the facade of indifference, Emily couldn't shake the nagging sense of responsibility that weighed heavily upon her heart. The realization dawned upon her with startling clarity – perhaps in her quest for solitude, she had inadvertently shut out the very connections that held the potential to enrich her life.

With each passing day, Emily found herself consumed by a growing sense of longing, a yearning to seek out the man she had dismissed so hastily and offer him the apology he deserved. For in the depths of her soul, she recognized the importance of acknowledging her mistakes and seeking reconciliation, even if it meant stepping outside the confines of her comfort zone.

As she navigated the ebb and flow of her daily routine, Emily remained vigilant, her eyes scanning the horizon in search of the familiar figure that had crossed her path. And though their encounter had been brief, she clung to the hope that one day, their paths would converge once more, affording her the opportunity to make amends and perhaps, in doing so, unlock the door to a connection that transcended the boundaries of time and circumstance.

As Emily returned from her errands, the warm rays of the sun enveloped her in their comforting embrace, casting a golden glow upon the bustling streets. Amidst the familiar hum of activity, her gaze was drawn to a solitary figure seated in the tranquil embrace of a nearby coffee shop. There, amidst the tranquil ambiance, sat a man whose gentle demeanor and familiar features stirred a sense of recognition within her soul.

A surge of excitement coursed through Emily's veins as she entertained the possibility that this could indeed be the same man she had encountered during her morning exercise. But as she stood at the threshold of possibility, uncertainty loomed large before her – how would she approach him, and what would she say?

With each step closer to the coffee shop, Emily's heart pounded with anticipation, her mind racing with a myriad of thoughts and possibilities. Should she summon the courage to approach him and offer an apology for her previous dismissal? Or would it be better to observe from afar, allowing fate to unfold its hand in due time?

As she weighed her options, Emily found herself torn between the desire to seize the moment and the fear of rejection that gnawed at the edges of her resolve. Yet amidst the swirling tempest of uncertainty, a quiet voice whispered within her soul, urging her to trust in the serendipitous nature of life's journey.

Summoning her courage, Emily took a tentative step forward, her heart buoyed by the hope that perhaps, in this unexpected encounter, lay the opportunity for reconciliation and connection. For in the tapestry of life, woven with threads of chance and possibility, she knew that sometimes, the greatest rewards awaited those brave enough to take the first step towards embracing the unknown.

As Emily drew nearer, she couldn't help but notice the striking features of the man she had glimpsed from afar. His slender frame exuded an effortless charm, while his captivating smile seemed to illuminate the entire coffee shop with its warmth and genuineness.

Summoning her courage, Emily approached him with a tentative smile, her heart fluttering with a mixture of nerves and anticipation. "Good afternoon," she greeted, her voice laced with a hint of uncertainty.

To her relief, the man returned her greeting with a smile that mirrored her own, his eyes twinkling with amusement and goodwill. Emboldened by his friendly demeanor, Emily found herself mustering the courage to offer her apology for their previous encounter.

With grace and kindness, the man accepted her apology with a gentle nod, his reassuring words washing away the lingering doubts that had plagued her conscience. "That was okay," he replied, his voice soft and reassuring.

In a gesture of hospitality, he extended an invitation for Emily to join him for a cup of coffee, a simple yet meaningful gesture that spoke volumes of his generosity and goodwill. With a grateful smile, Emily accepted his offer, her heart brimming with gratitude for the unexpected opportunity to set things right and perhaps, in doing so, forge a connection that transcended the boundaries of past misunderstandings.

As they settled into conversation over steaming cups of coffee, Emily felt a sense of kinship and camaraderie blossoming between them, like two souls finding solace in the serendipitous embrace of fate. And as they whiled away the hours lost in the rhythm of conversation, Emily couldn't help but marvel at the beauty of life's unexpected twists and turns, and the profound connections that await those brave enough to take a chance on the unknown.

As the moments stretched into hours, Emily and the man found themselves enveloped in a captivating conversation that flowed effortlessly between them. What had begun as a simple apology had blossomed into the beginnings of a profound friendship, rooted in mutual understanding and shared experiences.

With each passing moment, time seemed to lose its significance as they delved deeper into the intricacies of life, exchanging stories and insights with an intimacy that belied their brief acquaintance. They found themselves drawn to each other's experiences, their hearts resonating with the echoes of shared trials and triumphs.

There was a connection between them that transcended the physical realm, a bond forged in the quiet depths of their souls, where words ceased to be mere vessels of communication and instead became conduits of understanding and empathy.

In the midst of their conversation, Emily couldn't help but marvel at the synchronicity of their meeting, as though their souls had recognized each other from the moment they first locked eyes. Perhaps, she mused, their connection had been ordained by the universe, patiently waiting for the opportune moment to draw them together and kindle the flames of friendship that now burned brightly between them.

As they basked in the warmth of each other's company, Emily and the man found solace in the knowledge that they had found a kindred spirit in one another, a companion to accompany them on life's journey, through its twists and turns, its joys and sorrows.

For in the quiet sanctuary of their shared conversation, they discovered that true connection transcends the boundaries of time and space, weaving its threads through the fabric of destiny and drawing kindred souls together in a dance of serendipity and grace.

As the inexorable march of time pressed on, Emily and Mcking reluctantly acknowledged that their time together had come to an end. Despite the reluctance to part ways, they knew that the demands of life beckoned, pulling them in separate directions.

In the rush of the moment, amidst the effortless flow of conversation and the warmth of newfound camaraderie, they realized with a start that they hadn't exchanged names. It was a curious oversight, one that spoke volumes of the organic nature of their connection, forged in the serendipitous embrace of the present moment.

With a gentle smile, Mcking offered to drive Emily home, a gesture of kindness that warmed her heart even as she hesitated to accept, not wanting to burden him with the inconvenience. Yet as they made their way to his car, Emily was taken aback to discover that Mcking owned a luxurious Lincoln Navigator, a stark contrast to her initial assumption.

In that moment, the weight of her assumptions and preconceived notions bore down upon her, prompting Emily to offer yet another apology for her earlier misjudgment. In the quiet confines of the car, amidst the hum of the engine and the soft glow of streetlights, they found themselves sharing a moment of vulnerability and understanding, each seeking solace in the recognition of their shared humanity.

As they neared Emily's house, Mcking broke the silence with a warm smile, introducing himself in a gesture of openness and goodwill. In turn, Emily offered her own name, their smiles reflecting the unspoken bond that had formed between them in the span of a few fleeting hours.

With a sense of gratitude and anticipation, they exchanged contact information, a silent promise to stay connected in the days and weeks to come. And as Mcking pulled up to Emily's house, they bid each other farewell with a shared understanding that their paths would inevitably cross again, guided by the invisible hand of fate that had brought them together in the first place.

With a heart brimming with newfound joy and anticipation, Emily practically floated into her room, her footsteps light and buoyant as if she were walking on air. It was as if she had won the lottery of life, the elation of the day's unexpected encounter coursing through her veins like a euphoric melody.

In the sanctuary of her room, Emily couldn't contain the radiant smile that graced her lips, her entire being suffused with a sense of contentment that she had never experienced before. For the first time in her life, she felt truly happy, a sensation that washed over her like a warm embrace, banishing the shadows of doubt and loneliness that had once clouded her spirit. With a sense of hope and anticipation, Emily allowed herself to dream of the possibilities that lay ahead, of the friendship that had blossomed from the seeds of serendipity and connection. She dared to believe that this newfound bond would evolve into something meaningful and enduring, a source of comfort and companionship on the journey of life.

As she reflected on the events of the day, Emily felt a surge of gratitude for the unexpected gift that fate had bestowed upon her. With a silent prayer whispered into the ether, she surrendered herself to the unknown expanse of the future, trusting that whatever lay ahead would be guided by the invisible hand of destiny and the enduring power of friendship.

As Emily drifted off into the realm of dreams, her mind teetered on the precipice of uncertainty, caught between the allure of newfound connection and the haunting specter of past heartbreaks. Amidst the echoes of whispered doubts and fears, a question lingered in the air like a ghostly apparition - was this what she truly wanted?

In the silent recesses of her thoughts, Emily grappled with the weight of her own expectations and desires, wrestling with the age-old conundrum of whether love was worth the risk of pain. The stories of broken hearts that had echoed through the corridors of her consciousness loomed large before her, casting shadows of doubt upon the nascent spark of hope that flickered within her heart.

Was she drawn to Mcking for who he was, or was it the allure of his material possessions that held sway over her affections? The dichotomy between genuine connection and superficial attraction gnawed at her conscience, leaving her torn between the desire for companionship and the fear of being led astray by false promises.

And yet, amidst the labyrinth of her doubts and uncertainties, Emily remained steadfast in her belief that love, in its purest form, was worth the risk of pain. With a quiet resolve, she embraced the unknown with open arms, trusting that the journey towards love and fulfillment would reveal itself in due time.

For Emily knew that true happiness lay not in the absence of uncertainty or the guarantee of a pain-free existence, but in the courage to pursue one's heart's desires with unwavering faith and conviction. And as she drifted into slumber, a sense of peace washed over her, for she knew that whatever lay ahead, she would face it with a spirit of hope and resilience, guided by the unwavering light of her own inner truth.

As the first rays of dawn pierced through the curtains, Emily's eyes fluttered open, her heart aflutter with anticipation as she awaited the sound of her phone ringing, heralding the arrival of a call from Mcking. With bated breath, she lay in bed for what felt like an eternity, each passing moment filled with a sense of longing and expectation.

Hours stretched into eternity, yet the familiar chime of her phone remained conspicuously absent, leaving Emily feeling increasingly unsettled and disheartened. The silence weighed heavily upon her, casting a shadow over the bright promise of the new day.

"Why is he not calling?" she wondered aloud, her mind awash with a torrent of anxious thoughts and doubts. With each passing minute, the nagging sense of unease gnawed at her conscience, leaving her feeling adrift in a sea of uncertainty.

Unable to bear the silence any longer, Emily resolved to take matters into her own hands. With trembling fingers, she reached for her phone, her heart pounding with a mixture of trepidation and determination. Summoning her courage, she dialed Mcking's number, her pulse quickening with each ring of the phone.

As the line connected, Emily held her breath, her heart racing as she waited for Mcking to answer. And in that moment, amidst the crackle of static and the rush of her own heartbeat, she knew that whatever the outcome, she was ready to face it head-on, armed with the unwavering resolve to seek answers and clarity in the face of uncertainty.

As the call continued to go unanswered, frustration and worry gnawed at Emily's resolve, casting a shadow of doubt over her once-buoyant spirit. With each failed attempt to reach Mcking, her mind became a whirlwind of anxious thoughts and conjectures, each one more unsettling than the last.

"Did something happen to him on the way home?" she mused, her imagination conjuring images of unforeseen accidents and misfortunes that could have befallen him in the intervening hours since their parting.

Or perhaps, she wondered, a sinking feeling settling in the pit of her stomach, "Is he married, and unable to answer the call because his wife is close by?" The thought filled her with a sense of betrayal and disillusionment, shattering the fragile hope that had blossomed within her heart.

And then, the most haunting question of all echoed in the recesses of her mind, refusing to be silenced: "Is he ignoring me?" The mere possibility sent a shiver down Emily's spine, as she grappled with the notion that the connection she had felt with Mcking may have been nothing more than a fleeting illusion.

As the minutes stretched into hours, Emily found herself ensnared in a web of uncertainty and doubt, her heart torn between the desire for answers and the fear of facing the truth. With each passing moment, the weight of unanswered questions pressed upon her like a suffocating blanket, leaving her yearning for resolution and closure in the face of the unknown.

As Emily resigned herself to the rhythm of her daily activities, a sudden interruption shattered the monotony of her routine. With a sense of apprehension, she glanced at the unfamiliar number flashing on her phone screen, her brow furrowing with suspicion as she answered with a guarded tone.

To her surprise and dismay, the voice on the other end belonged to Mcking, offering an explanation for his prolonged absence and apologizing profusely for the misunderstanding. Yet, Emily couldn't shake the lingering sense of frustration that had taken root within her, the hours of unanswered calls weighing heavily upon her conscience.

With a mix of disappointment and indignation, Emily recounted her futile attempts to reach him, her voice tinged with the unmistakable edge of irritation. Mcking's shock at her revelation was palpable, his confusion mirroring her own as he adamantly denied receiving any missed calls from her.

As the realization dawned upon them both, a tense silence hung heavy in the air, punctuated only by the staccato rhythm of their breathing. The fragile threads of their newfound friendship strained under the weight of misunderstanding, threatening to unravel in the face of miscommunication and mistrust.

In a bid to unravel the mystery of the missed calls, Mcking implored Emily to recount the number she had been dialing. And as she hesitantly complied, a sense of disbelief washed over them both as they discovered the source of the confusion - a simple mix-up in the digits that had led to a series of missed connections and misunderstandings.

In the aftermath of their revelation, a sense of relief washed over Emily, mingled with a twinge of embarrassment at the misunderstanding that had threatened to derail their burgeoning friendship. With a newfound sense of understanding and clarity, they resolved to put the incident behind them, their bond strengthened by the shared experience of overcoming adversity and misunderstanding.

As Mcking proposed a date, Emily's heart soared with a mixture of excitement and anticipation. And so it was, their first date marked the beginning of a beautiful journey filled with laughter, shared dreams, and cherished memories.

As they navigated the ups and downs of their budding relationship, Emily and Mcking found solace in each other's presence, their bond growing stronger with each passing day. Despite the whispers of doubt and skepticism that surrounded their union, they remained steadfast in their belief that love, true and unwavering, would guide them through any obstacle that came their way.

For Emily, Mcking's love was a beacon of light in the darkness, a source of comfort and reassurance that banished the shadows of uncertainty and fear. And though many sought to cast their evil eyes upon their happiness, Emily refused to let their negativity dampen her spirits, knowing deep within her heart that Mcking would never intentionally hurt her, just as she would never do the same to him. In each other's arms, Emily and Mcking found sanctuary from the storms of life, their love a refuge amidst the chaos and uncertainty of the world. And as they embarked on this journey together, hand in hand, they knew that no matter what the future held, they would face it together, united in the unbreakable bond of love and devotion.

As their love continued to blossom and flourish, Emily and Mcking found themselves drawn ever closer, their hearts intertwined in a tapestry of shared dreams and aspirations. And so, on a fateful day filled with love and anticipation, Mcking took Emily's hand in his own and dropped to one knee, his eyes shining with unbridled devotion as he professed his undying love and commitment.

With tears of joy streaming down her cheeks, Emily could scarcely believe the depth of emotion that surged within her heart at Mcking's heartfelt proposal. In that magical moment, surrounded by the echoes of their shared laughter and the gentle caress of the breeze, she knew with unwavering certainty that this was the man she wanted to spend the rest of her life with.

And so, with a resounding "yes" that echoed through the very depths of her soul, Emily accepted Mcking's proposal, sealing their bond in an unbreakable promise of love and devotion. In that moment, their hearts beat as one, united in a shared vision of a future filled with love, peace, and understanding.

As they looked forward to the journey that lay ahead, Emily and Mcking were filled with an overwhelming sense of gratitude and joy, knowing that their union was blessed by the hand of fate itself. For in each other's arms, they had found not only love, but also a companion to share in life's joys and sorrows, triumphs and challenges.

And so, with hearts full of love and eyes shining with hope, Emily and Mcking embarked on the next chapter of their journey together, their love shining as brightly as the stars in the night sky, illuminating the path that lay before them with the promise of a lifetime of happiness and fulfillment.

Despite the envious glances and whispered doubts that surrounded their union, Emily and Mcking remained steadfast in their commitment to each other, refusing to let negativity dim the light of their love. With unwavering determination and resilience, they forged ahead, their hearts beating in unison as they embarked on the journey towards their happily ever after.

And so, amidst the skepticism and doubt of friends and family, Emily and Mcking stood unwavering in their love, their bond unbreakable and their resolve unshakable. As they exchanged vows of love and devotion in a beautiful ceremony surrounded by their nearest and dearest, the air was filled with the sweet melody of joy and celebration.

Their wedding day was a testament to the power of love to triumph over adversity, a joyous occasion filled with laughter, tears, and moments of pure, unadulterated bliss. Surrounded by the love and support of their loved ones, Emily and Mcking danced the night away, their hearts overflowing with gratitude and happiness as they embarked on this new chapter of their lives together. In the end, their love proved stronger than any doubt or negativity that sought to undermine it, shining brightly as a beacon of hope and inspiration for all who witnessed their union. And as they looked ahead to the future, hand in hand, Emily and Mcking knew that together, they could weather any storm and conquer any obstacle, their love serving as a guiding light to illuminate their path towards a lifetime of happiness and fulfillment.

Indeed, the journey of marriage is often fraught with challenges and obstacles, testing the strength and resilience of the bonds that unite two souls in love. For Emily and Mcking, their union was no exception, as they navigated the ebbs and flows of life together, facing each challenge with unwavering determination and steadfast commitment to one another.

From the trials of everyday life to the unexpected curveballs that fate threw their way, Emily and Mcking stood united, facing adversity with courage and grace. Theirs was a journey marked by perseverance, resilience, and an unwavering belief in the power of love to conquer all obstacles.

Through the storms of life, they found strength in each other's arms, drawing closer together in the face of adversity and emerging stronger and more resilient than ever before. And as they weathered the ups and downs of marriage, they discovered that true love is not just about the moments of joy and happiness, but also about the unwavering support and commitment to stand by each other's side through thick and thin.

Their story serves as a testament to the enduring power of love, reminding us that true happiness is not found in the absence of challenges, but in the courage to face them together, hand in hand. And while not every love story may have a fairy tale ending, Emily and Mcking's journey reminds us that with determination, resilience, and unwavering faith in each other, true love can indeed conquer all.

THE END.

What is love? Is it merely the fleeting rush of adrenaline, igniting our senses with a blaze of passion? Or perhaps it's a seductive mirage, a tantalizing illusion we chase relentlessly? But dare we ask: Is love real? These questions, like ghosts in the dark, haunt the corridors of our minds, whispering secrets of desire and longing. With each beat of our hearts, we search for answers amidst the chaos of emotion, navigating the treacherous waters of the human soul. For love is not merely a question to ponder—it's a journey to embark upon, a labyrinth of ecstasy and agony where we may find the ultimate truth that eludes us all.

Love, a formidable force that defies the boundaries of tribe, ethnicity, and even the spectrum of human emotions. It is an enigmatic power, capable of transcending the confines of the known universe. Love possesses a transformative essence, reshaping lives with its undeniable sway. Its manifestation can be witnessed in the unwavering gaze of a mother towards her child, an unyielding bond that surpasses comprehension. Deep within the recesses of our hearts, this inexplicable force takes root, defying quantification by any earthly instrument. Love, an ethereal phenomenon that permeates the very fabric of existence, defying explanation and commanding reverence.

The misconception of love, a treacherous labyrinth that ensnares countless souls, leading them down paths of illusion and deceit, ultimately culminating in the mournful ballads of regret. Fueling this deception are the enchanting tales of Romeo and Juliet, Cinderella, and a myriad of other fairytales, weaving dreams of happily ever afters into the fabric of our consciousness. Oh, how we yearn for the fairy tale endings crafted within these stories, where true love conquers all and adversity bends to the will of destiny. But reality, cruel and unforgiving, presents a different game altogether.

In reality, there are no enchanted princess kisses capable of transforming frogs into princely heroes. Instead, we are confronted with the harsh truths of life, where love is often marred by imperfections and complexities. The romanticized narratives of fairy tales offer little solace in the face of heartbreak and disappointment. Yet, amidst the rubble of shattered dreams, there lies a glimmer of hope—a chance to rewrite our own story, to embrace the messy, imperfect reality of love, and to find beauty in its raw authenticity.

For true love, though devoid of fairy tale enchantment, possesses a power far greater—the power to endure, to heal, and to transcend the confines of fantasy, leaving an indelible mark on the human spirit.

Indeed, the quest for true love can lead to tears of the most bitter kind if one neglects to nurture love for oneself. The first crucial step on this journey is not merely to adorn oneself with superficial charms, but rather to cultivate a deep and abiding love for the very essence of who we are. For without self-love as our foundation, no amount of external affection can fill the void within.

To embark upon the path of self-love is to embark upon a journey of profound introspection and acceptance. It requires embracing our flaws and imperfections with open arms, recognizing that our worthiness of love is inherent, not contingent upon external validation. In the absence of self-love, we become like parched souls wandering a desert, endlessly seeking sustenance from others yet finding only mirages of fulfillment.

But when we learn to love ourselves unconditionally, we become like mighty oaks, firmly rooted in our own sense of worthiness. We no longer rely on others to define our value or validate our existence. Instead, we radiate a magnetic self-assurance that draws love and admiration towards us like moths to a flame.

So let us heed this vital truth: the journey to true love begins not in the arms of another, but within the chambers of our own hearts. Let us water the seeds of self-love with kindness, compassion, and unwavering acceptance, knowing that only then can we truly experience the depths of love's boundless magic.

Emily's relentless quest for love always seemed to culminate in a familiar pattern of pain and heartache, leaving her battered and bruised by the harsh realities of romance. Despite her brilliance and intellect, she found herself perpetually ensnared in a cycle of disappointment and despair. For Emily, the pursuit of love was like navigating a labyrinthine maze, fraught with pitfalls and dead ends, each wrong turn leading her further away from the elusive prize she sought.

It wasn't that Emily lacked charm or allure; on the contrary, her intellect and wit often captivated those around her. But beneath the facade of confidence lay a deep-seated insecurity, a gnawing self-doubt that whispered cruel taunts in the quiet corners of her mind. She was her own harshest critic, forever measuring herself against impossible standards of perfection and falling short.

Yet amidst the wreckage of shattered dreams, Emily found herself at a crossroads—a moment of reckoning that demanded she confront the demons that haunted her soul. It was a journey of self-discovery, a voyage into the depths of her own heart where she unearthed buried truths and confronted long-held fears. Through tears and turmoil, she began to unravel the tangled web of her insecurities, slowly but surely learning to embrace the flawed, imperfect beauty of her own humanity. And in that moment of self-acceptance, Emily found the key to unlocking the door to true love—not in the arms of another, but within the depths of her own being. For it was only when she learned to love herself—fully, fiercely, unconditionally—that she was able to break free from the cycle of pain and embrace the boundless possibilities that lay before her.

Indeed, the quest for true love often begins with lofty expectations and rigid criteria, as we cling to the belief that our ideal partner must fit a predetermined mold. Yet, time and again, we find ourselves disillusioned by the harsh reality that love does not conform to our neatly crafted fantasies. True love, it seems, is a wild and unpredictable force, unfazed by the constraints of our desires.

For true love does not come to us on the wings of our expectations; rather, it arrives when we least expect it, in the most unexpected of forms. It is not bound by the checkboxes we meticulously tick off on our mental checklist, but rather by the openness and vulnerability of our hearts. It is in those moments of unguarded authenticity that we find ourselves drawn to the most unlikely of souls, recognizing in them a kindred spirit that defies rational explanation.

In the end, we come to realize that love knows no boundaries, no criteria, no rules. It is a force of nature, untamed and untethered, flowing freely wherever it pleases. To truly experience love in all its raw beauty, we must release ourselves from the shackles of our own selfishness and embrace the unpredictable journey that lies before us. For only then can we open our hearts to the possibility of finding true love in the most unexpected of places, with the most unlikely of companions.

Absolutely, it's a profound truth that greatness isn't always packaged in the flashy exterior we might expect. In the same vein, folly doesn't necessarily come wrapped in a dull, unassuming guise. It's a lesson worth remembering: appearances can be deceiving, and true worth lies far beyond the superficial.

Many have made the mistake of overlooking greatness because it didn't come in the expected form, dismissing it as unworthy or insignificant. Yet, within those underestimated individuals often lies a depth of character, talent, and potential waiting to be discovered. By judging solely based on outward appearances, we risk missing out on the opportunity to be in the presence of greatness.

Conversely, some have been deceived by superficial charms, mistaking them for genuine greatness, only to realize later that they've settled for mediocrity. It's a reminder that the allure of the surface can blind us to the substance within.

So let us heed this wisdom and approach each individual with an open heart and a discerning mind, recognizing that true greatness often lies beneath the surface, waiting to be uncovered and appreciated. Let us not be swayed by appearances or titles, but instead, let us seek out the qualities that truly define greatness: integrity, humility, kindness, and resilience. For in doing so, we may just find ourselves in the company of greatness beyond our wildest dreams.

It's true that society often has our best interests in mind, but it's also guilty of heaping on pressures that can feel suffocating at times. When you're single, there's a constant barrage of inquiries about when you'll find a partner, settle down, and start a family. And once you've crossed that threshold into marriage, the questions don't stop—they merely shift focus.

Suddenly, the pressure to procreate becomes overwhelming, as if society has appointed itself the keeper of your biological clock. But even when you've brought a child into the world, the inquiries continue unabated. When will you enroll them in school? When will you have another baby? It's as if the decision-making power over your life has been handed over to the collective whims of society.

But here's the thing: society doesn't pay the bills or bear the burdens of our choices. It doesn't feel the weight of our struggles or the joy of our triumphs. So why should we let its expectations dictate the course of our lives?

Let us remember that our journey is our own to navigate, and we owe no explanations to anyone but ourselves. Whether we choose to follow society's script or carve out our own path, let it be a decision made from a place of authenticity and self-awareness, rather than succumbing to the pressures of external expectations. For in the end, it's our happiness and fulfillment that matter most, not society's checklist of milestones.

Societal constructs should never be allowed to burden us or dictate the course of our lives. In the realm of relationships, it's crucial to remember that it's not a competition. Marriage isn't a race to the altar, nor is it a contest to see who can throw the grandest wedding.

Relationships are deeply personal journeys, unique to each individual and couple. They're about forging connections based on love, respect, and mutual understanding, rather than trying to outdo one another in a societal game of one-upmanship.

The size of your wedding or the timing of your marriage doesn't determine the strength or validity of your relationship. What truly matters is the bond you share with your partner, the love and support you offer each other, and the commitment to weather life's challenges together.

So let's cast off the shackles of societal expectations and embrace the beauty of love in its purest form. Let's celebrate each other's milestones with genuine joy and support, knowing that true happiness lies not in comparison, but in the depth and authenticity of our connections with one another.

As I draw this reflection to a close, it's crucial to acknowledge that true love is characterized by understanding, compromise, and forgiveness. In the intricate tapestry of relationships, there are bound to be struggles and challenges. Yet, it is the unwavering commitment and resilience to persevere through the storms that lead us to a place of greater strength and unity.

Love isn't a smooth sailing journey devoid of obstacles; it's a tumultuous voyage marked by peaks and valleys. But it is in the midst of these trials that we discover the depth of our bond, the strength of our resolve, and the power of our love.

Through understanding, we bridge the divide between hearts, fostering empathy and compassion for one another's experiences. Through compromise, we navigate the complexities of differing perspectives and find common ground upon which to build our shared future. And through forgiveness, we release the weight of past grievances and embrace the freedom to move forward with renewed hope and trust. So let us remember that true love isn't about avoiding conflict or glossing over imperfections; it's about facing adversity head-on, hand in hand, and emerging stronger and more united on the other side. It's about embracing the journey with all its twists and turns, knowing that it is our unwavering commitment to each other that will ultimately lead us to a place of enduring happiness and fulfillment.

And finally, as we conclude, it's essential to leave behind the baggage of our past experiences. Who you've had in your life is not the same as who you have now. Each person is unique, with their own quirks, strengths, and vulnerabilities.

To treat a new relationship as if it were a continuation of past experiences is to do a disservice to both yourself and your partner. It's like replaying an old record, destined to produce the same tired tune. Instead, approach each new relationship with a fresh perspective, turning the page to a new chapter in your life's story.

It's unfair to bleed on someone who never hurt you, to burden them with the scars of wounds they didn't inflict. Let each new connection be a clean slate, untainted by the shadows of the past. Allow yourself to love and be loved without the fear of reprisal or the weight of past transgressions.

So, as you embark on this journey of love and connection, remember to leave behind the ghosts of yesterday and embrace the promise of tomorrow. For in doing so, you open yourself up to the possibility of finding true happiness and fulfillment in the arms of someone who sees you for who you truly are, not who you once were.

Thank you for taking time to read this piece. I hope you found it helpful and enjoyable, while also gaining insight from the lessons it imparts. May your journey be filled with love, growth, and fulfillment. Have a fruitful love life.

Mcking Pneuma.

www.ingramcontent.com/pod-product-compliance
Lightning Source LLC
Chambersburg PA
CBHW040230240726

48664CB00001B/81